OXFORDSHIRE COUNTY COUNCIL
Woodeaton Manor School
Woodeaton
Oxford OX3 9TS
Telephone: Oxford 58722

Life in Europe

DEBORAH ELLIOTT

Wayland

Titles in the Into Europe series include:
**Energy
Environment
Europe's History
Farming
Holidays and Holidaymakers
Industry
Transport**

Picture Acknowledgements
Associated Press/Topham 41; Allan Cash Ltd. 14, 19, 20, 21, 24 (top); Cephas (Stuart Boreham) 28, (Mick Rock) 43; Chapel Studios 24 (bottom); Eye Ubiquitous frontispiece, (Mike Feeney) 17, 40; G.S.F. Picture Library 11; Hutchison Library 5 (Nancy Durrell McKennna), 10, 16, 27, 44; Oskar Radelli 7, 22, 30; Tony Stone Worldwide cover, (bottom, Joe Cornish) (top, Anthony Friedmann) , (Tom Raymond) 4, (Joe Cornish) 8, (Stephen Johnson) 12, (Colin Prior) 23, (David H. Endersbee) 26, (Francois Puyplat) 27 (top), (Mike King) 31, (Charlie Waite) 38; Wayland Picture Library 15; Zefa 9, 13, 18, 25, 31, 37 (bottom). All artwork is by Malcolm Walker.

Designed by Malcolm Walker

Text based on *Living in Europe* in the Europe series published in 1992.

First published in 1994 by Wayland (Publishers) Limited
61 Western Road, Hove, East Sussex BN3 1JD

© Copyright Wayland (Publishers) Limited

British Library Cataloguing in Publication Data
Elliott, Deborah
 Life in Europe. - (Into Europe Series)
 I. Title II. Series
 940

ISBN 0 7502 1045 1

Typeset by Kudos
Printed and bound by G.Canale & C.S.p.A. in Turin, Italy

Contents

Living in Europe 4
Houses and shops 16
In the country 22
Towns and cities 28
How we live 38
Glossary 46
More information 47
Index 48

Cover pictures:
(top)   Busy shoppers in the fashionable Champs Elysées in Paris.
(bottom)   This narrow street is in Villefranche in Provence, France. It is typical of the streets in the towns and villages of France. French people, like Italians, live mostly in apartments with balconies, where washing can be hung out to dry.

Living in Europe

Today, most countries in Europe have good health care. This means that people live longer now than in the past. ▼

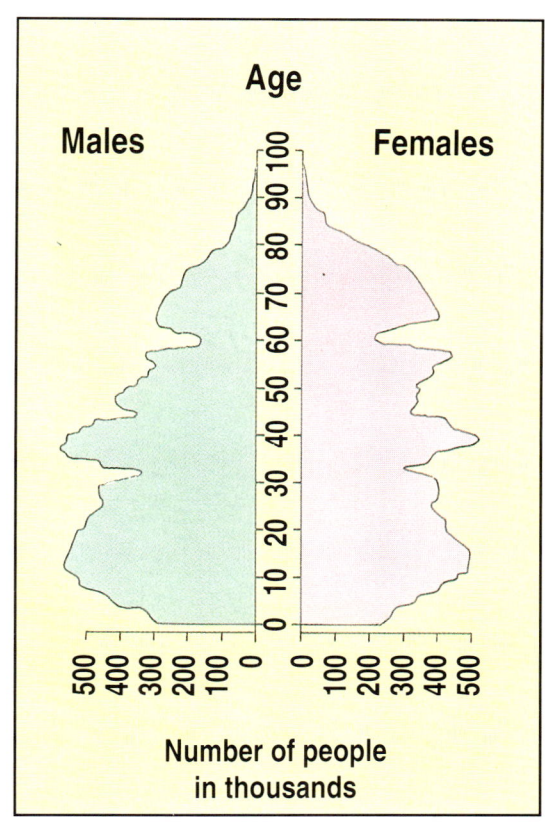

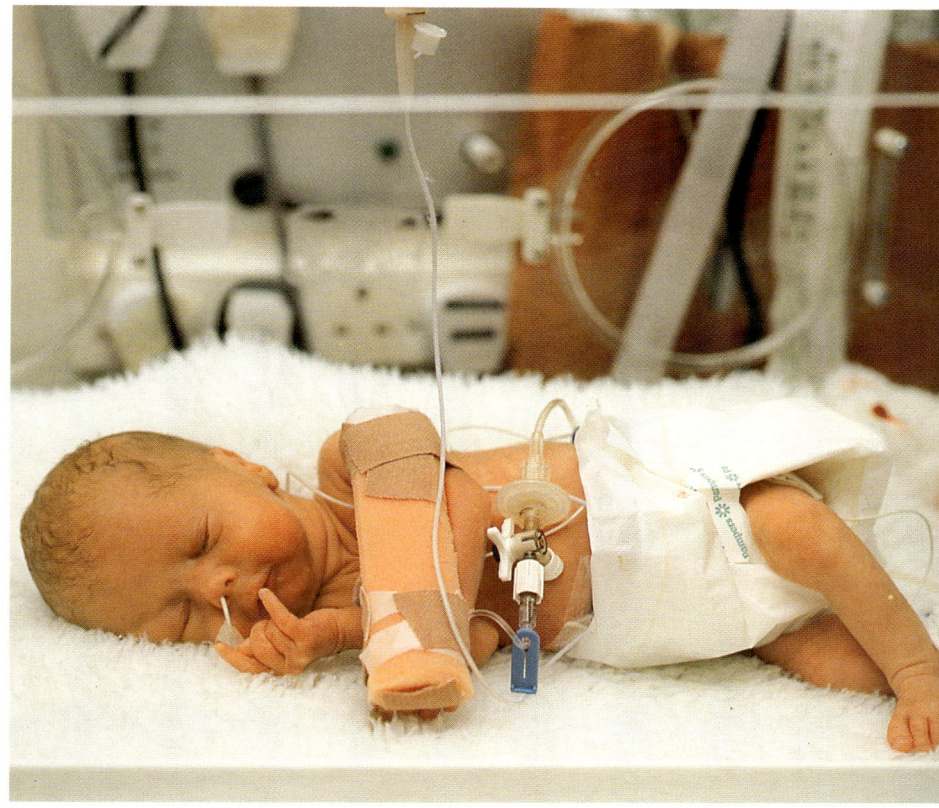

▲ There are a number of different ways of finding out information about the people living in a particular country.

The diagram above is a population pyramid. It tells us the age of all the people living in Germany.

▲ This baby was born prematurely (early). He is being cared for in a hospital high-tech care unit. Special equipment is used to help him breathe and to make sure his heart is beating properly.

Years ago, the baby would probably have died because none of this equipment was available.

The countries of Europe have different landscapes and climates. These affect the type of jobs people do, the way they live and the homes they live in.

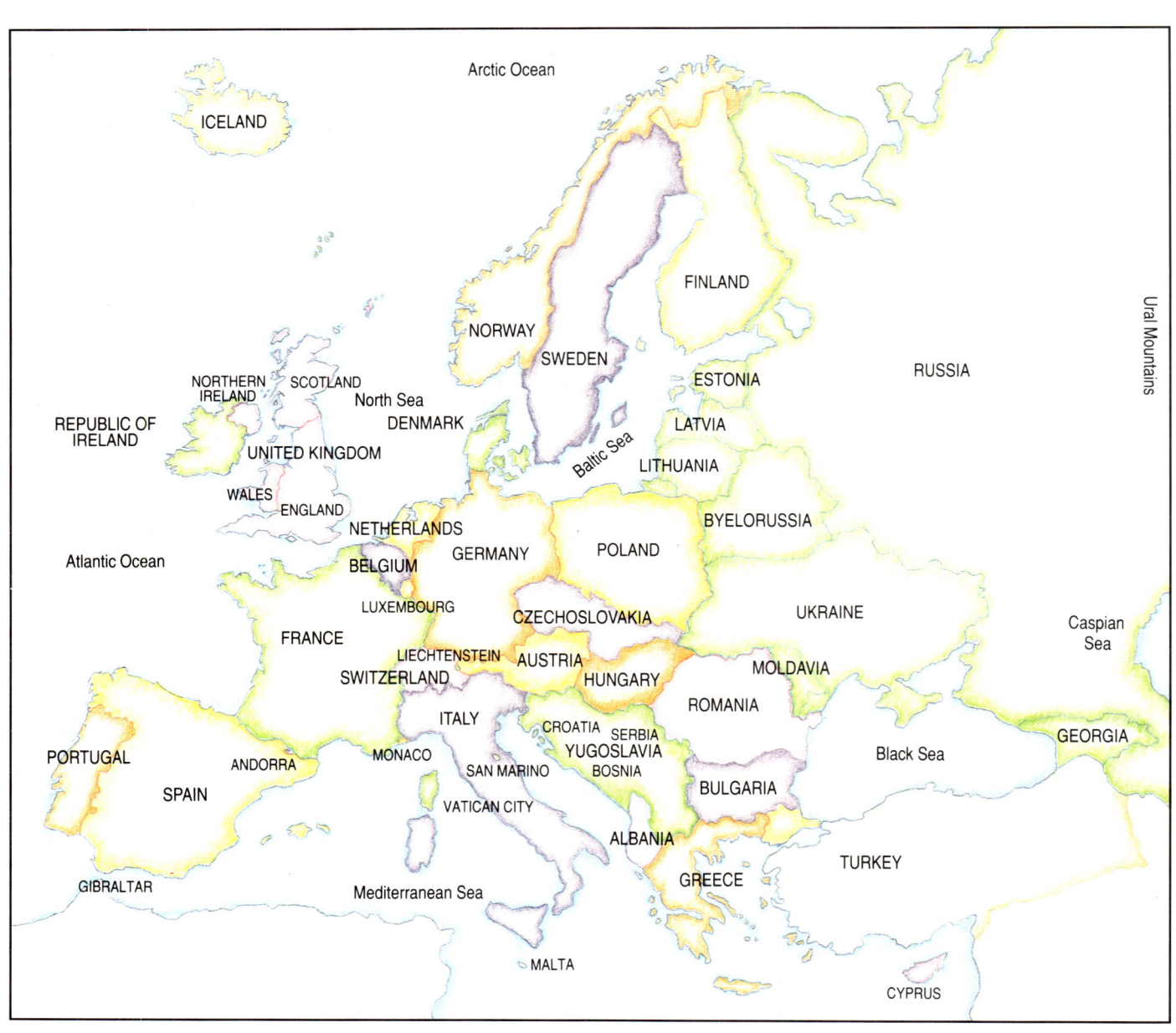

▲ *The countries of Europe.*

Italy is a country in southern Europe with beautiful countryside, mountains, lakes, rivers, hills and grassy plains. There are many pretty villages, towns and cities in Italy, too.

The main industries in Italy are car making, steel making and chemicals. These are found mainly in the richer north of the country.

Most schools in Italy are run by the government. School starts at 8 o' clock in the morning and finishes at lunchtime. Children have to go to school on Saturday mornings, too. ▶

▼ *Much of the Italian countryside is used for farming. Here, in the Apennine Mountains, in central Italy, cattle and sheep graze, and farmers produce milk, butter, cheese and beef.*

▲ *This busy seaside resort is part of the Côte d'Azure in the south of France. Hundreds of thousands of people come from all over the world to visit the area.*

Europe has many beautiful seaside resorts, especially parts of southern Europe which lie on the Mediterranean Sea.

Most people who live in these areas work in the tourist industry – hotels, restaurants, shops and nightclubs, for example.

▲ *Many of the people who live in this housing estate in Moscow, in Russia, work in the factories and power stations you can see in the background, pumping out dirty smoke and pollution into the air.*

People who live in Europe's cities have to deal with such problems as lack of housing, pollution, too much traffic and lots of noise.

So why do more people in Europe choose to live in cities than in the countryside?

Cities have more shops, factories and industries, which means more jobs. There are more hospitals, schools, libraries and better shops, theatres, cinemas and places to visit.

▼ *Cities have more nursery schools, which is good news for working mothers.*

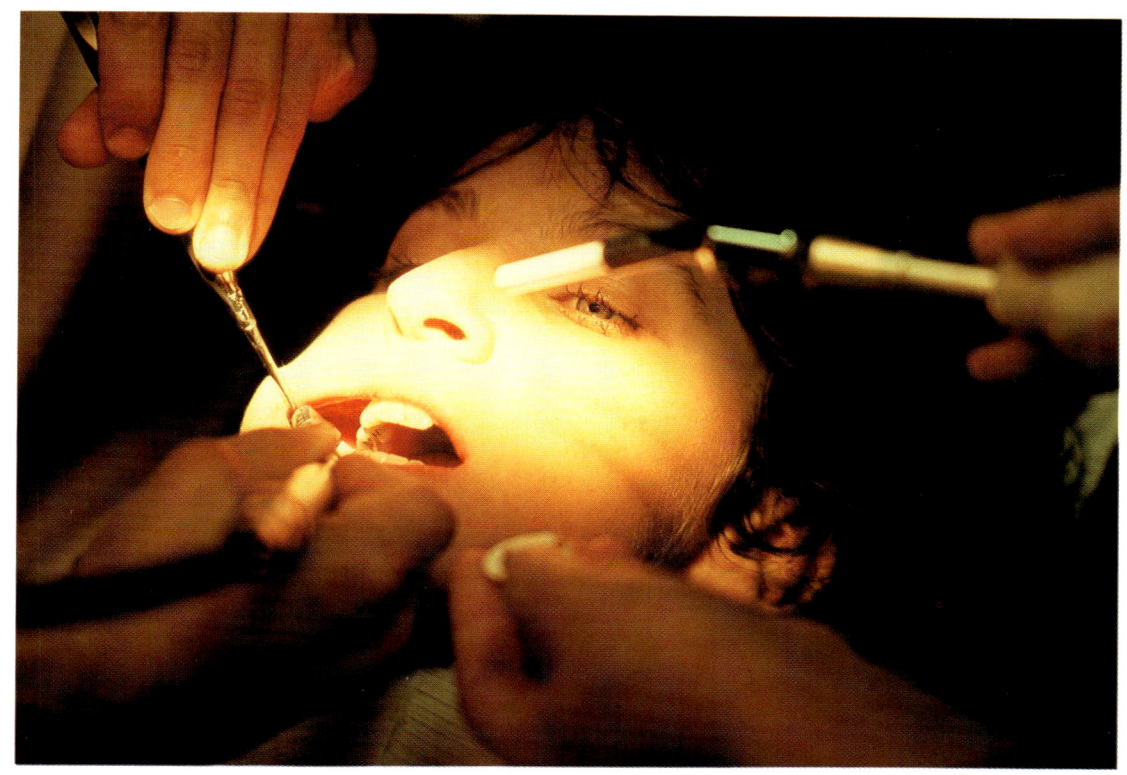

▲ *There are more hospitals in cities than in country areas.*

◀ *Large shopping centres like this have lots of different shops all in one building. They are found in and around big cities and are very popular with shoppers.*

Despite the advantages of life in Europe's cities, a number of people choose to live in the country. This is because there is less pollution, noise and crime than in towns and cities and, usually, the way of life is less stressful.

Some people have no choice about where they live. Guest workers are people who have moved to other countries in search of work. Some find themselves treated as 'outsiders' in their new homes, where they do not speak the language or share the culture. Many guest workers end up doing jobs that other people do not want to do.

▼ *Most of Germany's guest workers are from Turkey.*

▼ *Germany has a large number of guest workers. This chart shows which countries the workers come from.*

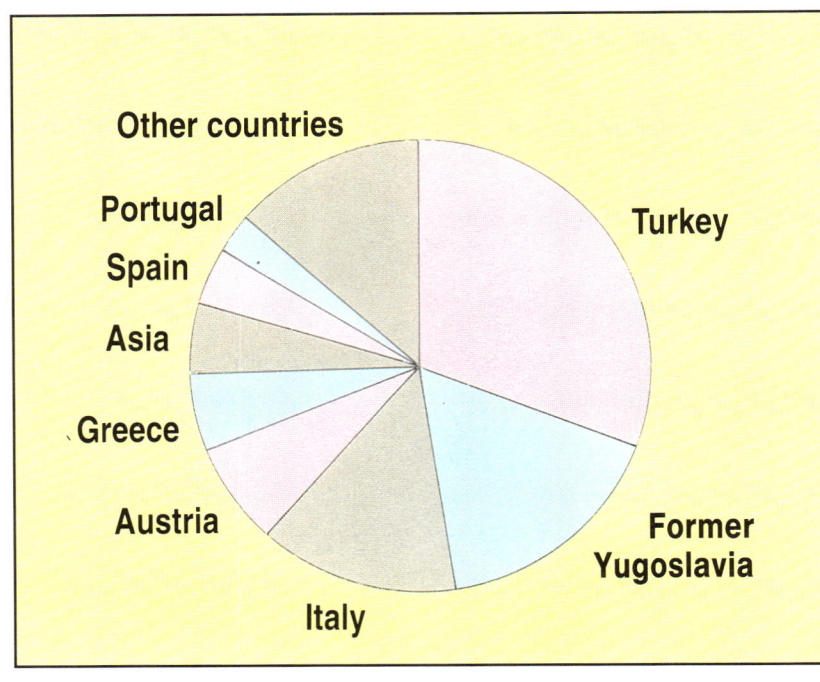

Raoul was born in Mozambique, a country in Africa. He moved to Portugal to find work about four years ago.

Up until 1975 Mozambique was ruled by the government of Portugal. Yet Raoul has been made to feel unwelcome by some Portugese people, who feel he has 'stolen' a job. ▶

Most guest workers find life very difficult in their new homes. Many have to live in very poor conditions.

Guest workers are a part of Europe and should be treated fairly and with respect. They bring new cultures and languages to a continent brimming with lots of different people.

Houses and shops

▲ *In towns and cities in Italy, most people live in blocks of flats. Many flats have balconies where washing can be hung out to dry.*

People need homes which keep them warm in cold weather and cool in hot weather, and where they can feel safe.

▼ *Farmhouses like this can be found in country areas of the Netherlands. The steep-sided roof was built specially to get rid of heavy winter snow.*

Usually, houses in hot Mediterranean countries, such as Spain, southern Italy, Portugal and Greece, are painted white to reflect the heat from the Sun.

▼ *Houses on the pretty Greek island of Mykonos have flat roofs. People can sleep on the roofs at night to keep cool. Houses have lots of windows, too, so that cooling breezes blow through the rooms.*

Are they houses, or part of the rolling hills?

These farmhouses in Iceland have turf covering the roofs. This stops heat from escaping in the freezing cold winters. ▶

The shape and design of the houses in Europe are quite different. They depend on the weather, how much money people have, available materials and traditional patterns.

Houses in Europe are usually made of materials which are found locally and can be got hold of easily.

▲ *Some of the delicious cheeses sold at the Alkmaar market in the Netherlands.*

In countries like France, Spain, Portugal, Greece and Italy, people like to buy fresh food at markets where they can choose the fruit, vegetables, cheese, meat and fish.

Although markets are popular, most Europeans prefer to shop at supermarkets, or at huge shopping centres. These are usually found outside town centres, where parking is easier.

Shopping centres, like this one in England, make shopping easier because all you need is under one roof. This is helpful in cold or wet weather! ▶

In the country

▲ *In country areas of Italy, people live in houses or farmhouses. Families have gardens where they can grow fruit and vegetables, and keep chickens and goats.*

Despite the cleaner environment in the country, more and more young people are leaving and moving to towns. They go to study at colleges or universities, and to find jobs.

The governments of some European countries are trying to encourage people to stay in the country. They are building new roads, hospitals, schools and houses.

▼ *It is hard to imagine a more beautiful part of the world than Lannoch Moor in Scotland. But very few people choose to live here because they have to travel long distances to hospitals and schools.*

◀ *Look at the run-down cottage at the front of this photograph. It is in County Galway in the west of Ireland.*

New houses and bungalows, like the one in the background, are being built throughout the Irish countryside.

Many people in Europe work in towns or cities and live in the countryside. They are called commuters, because they travel long distances to work.

New housing estates are being built in villages and country areas. ▶

24

Russia

Look at the map of Europe on page 6. You will see that Russia is a huge country. It has many different landscapes, but most of the land is countryside.

About thirty years ago, almost two-thirds of Russian people lived in country areas and worked in farming. Today less than one-third live in the country.

People are leaving the countryside for the better health care, schools and job opportunities in towns and cities.

▲ *This is the old town of Buchara in Uzbekistan. Many of the houses in the area are in very poor condition.*

Although, generally, there are more houses in towns than in the country, it does not always mean the standard of housing is good.

▲ *Young people find towns and cities more exciting places to live than country areas. There are more and better shops, cinemas, theatres, restaurants and night clubs.*

◀ *This is the sea front in Eastbourne on the south coast of England. People move to places like Eastbourne because they prefer the milder climate and slower pace of life.*

Because governments are making living conditions better in country areas, more people are choosing to live there. Commuters and retired people buy most of the new houses.

However, this means that house prices are high in many areas and few local people can afford to buy new homes.

Towns and cities

▲ *There are more people living and working in Europe's cities than ever before. More people means more traffic which, of course, means more traffic jams!*

Towns in Europe are growing day by day as more people come in search of work, and as businesses and industries develop.

House prices are very high which means that fewer people can buy their own homes. However, rents for flats, houses and offices are also high.

The governments of many European countries are looking at ways to make life better in towns and cities.

▼ *Look at the chart below. Can you see that more Germans than Britons live in flats? More Britons own their homes.*

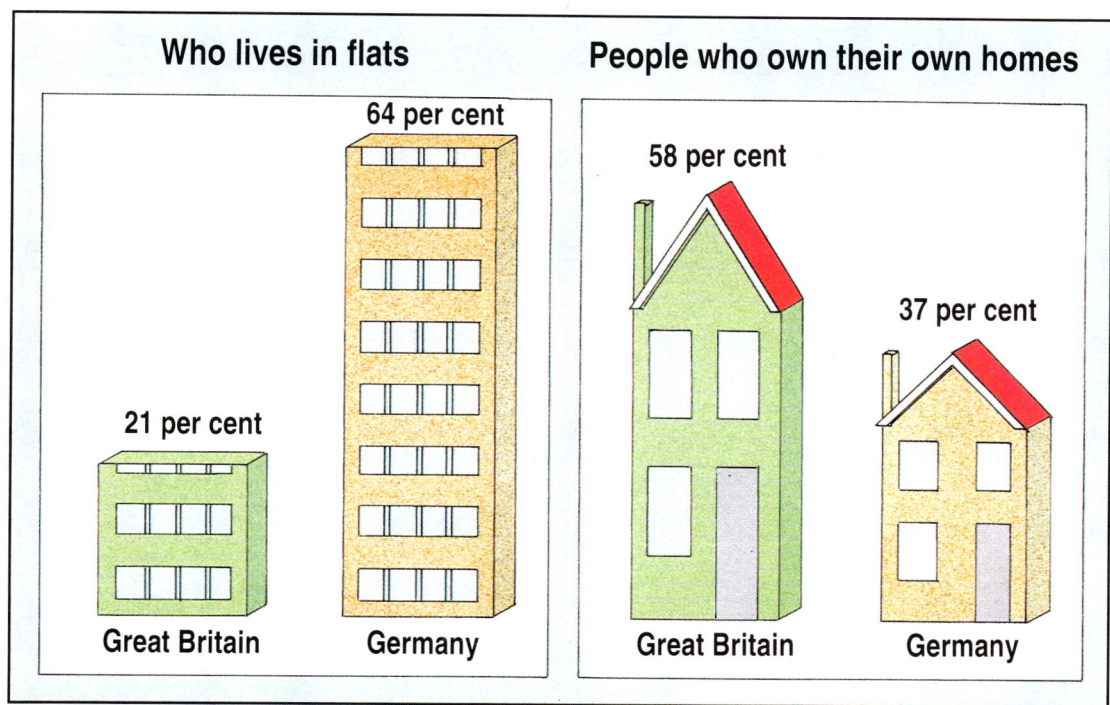

◀ *This diagram shows the percentage of houses in certain European countries with inside toilets.*

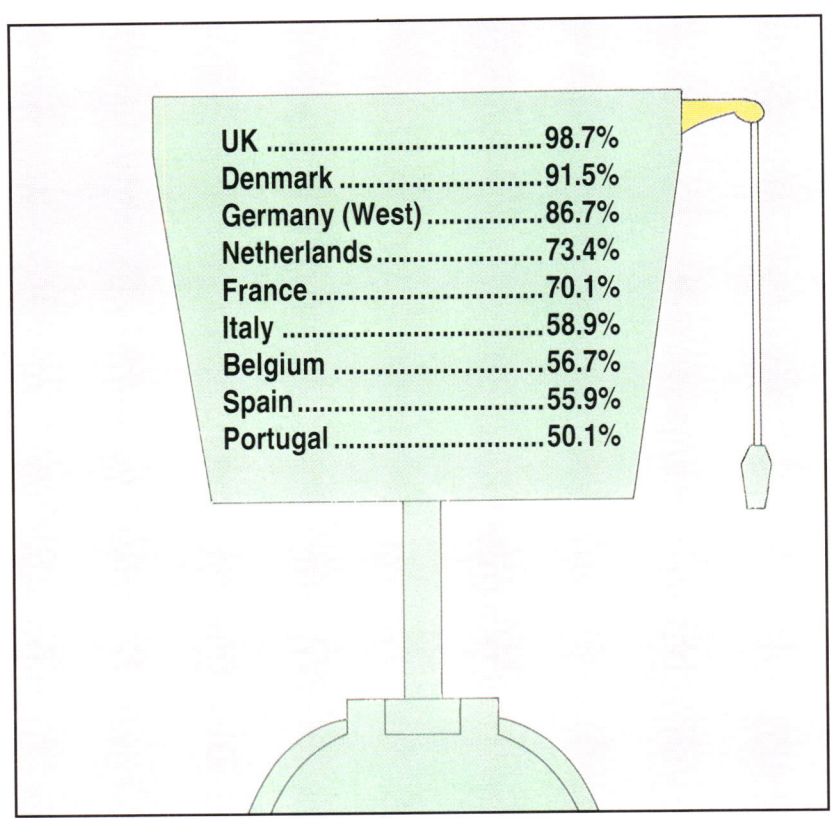

UK	98.7%
Denmark	91.5%
Germany (West)	86.7%
Netherlands	73.4%
France	70.1%
Italy	58.9%
Belgium	56.7%
Spain	55.9%
Portugal	50.1%

▼ *Today, developers are taking care to make new buildings look attractive. In the past, office blocks in city centres looked cold, grim and ugly.*

The marathon races held every year in the streets of European cities attract many tourists. ▶

▼ Most European towns and cities are steeped in history. Visitors flock to see the interesting buildings and architecture. This is part of the historic Old Town in Samarkand in Uzbekistan.

The Ruhr

The map below is of the Ruhr, a large industrial area in Germany. People living in the Ruhr work in coal mining and steel making. Although these industries provide plenty of jobs, they also cause a lot of pollution.

About seventy years ago, a plan was worked out to clean up the Ruhr. There are now five 'Green Areas' which lie between the cities in the area. These have been planted with trees and flowers.

There are also five parks with swimming pools, health clubs and open spaces for sport. All this has made the Ruhr a much better place to live.

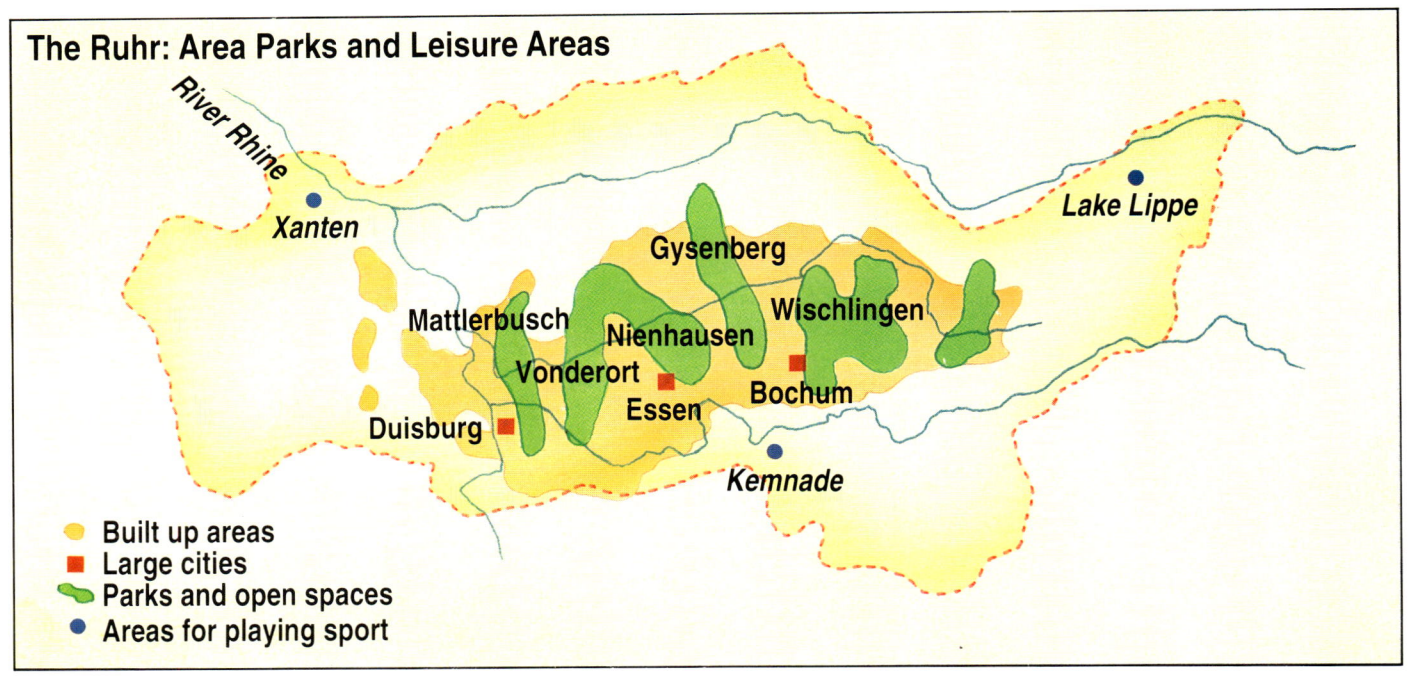

New towns

All over Europe, new towns are being built to solve the problem of overcrowding in cities.

Lelystad in the Netherlands is a new town. It is built on land which was once covered by the sea.

Most people living in the town moved from Amsterdam. Much of the housing in Amsterdam was old and in poor condition, and has since been knocked down.

There are four main housing areas in Lelystad. Traffic is not allowed in any of the areas, which cuts down pollution.

Solntsevo is about 30 kilometres from Moscow in Russia

On page 25 we read how many Russian people were leaving the countryside and going to live in cities like Moscow. However, there is not enough housing in the cities for everyone. So, new towns like Solntsevo are being built.

The new towns have shops, schools and parks. They are like small villages.

The new towns do not have enough jobs for everyone though, so some people have to travel to cities to work.

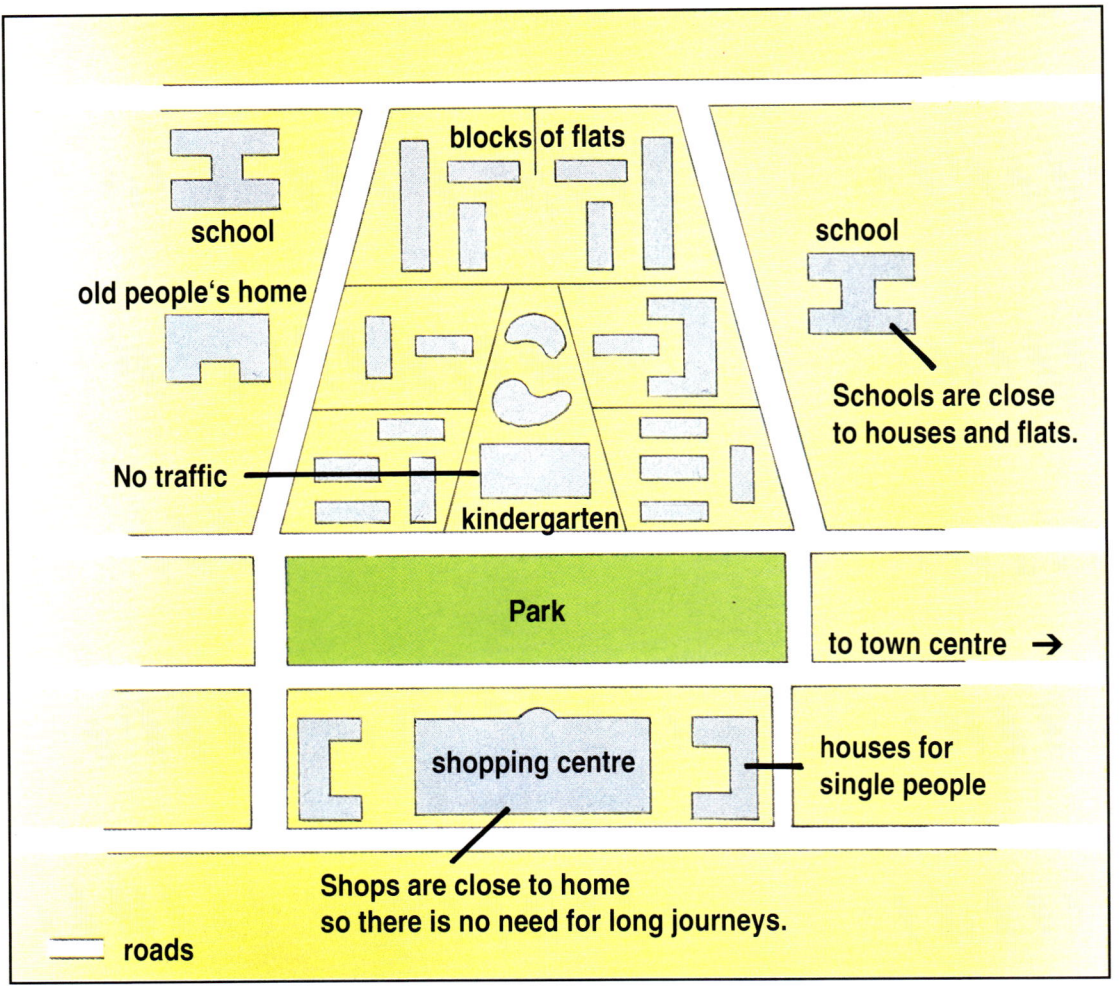

The diagram above shows an example of the layout of a new town in Russia.

Although they were built with schools and shops, the towns have become so big that there are not enough services for all the people living in them.

Randstad, Holland 1900

Randstad, Holland now

Scale 0 — 50km

- Towns
- Green areas
- Fresh water
- dams

Amsterdam, The Hague, Rotterdam, Utrecht

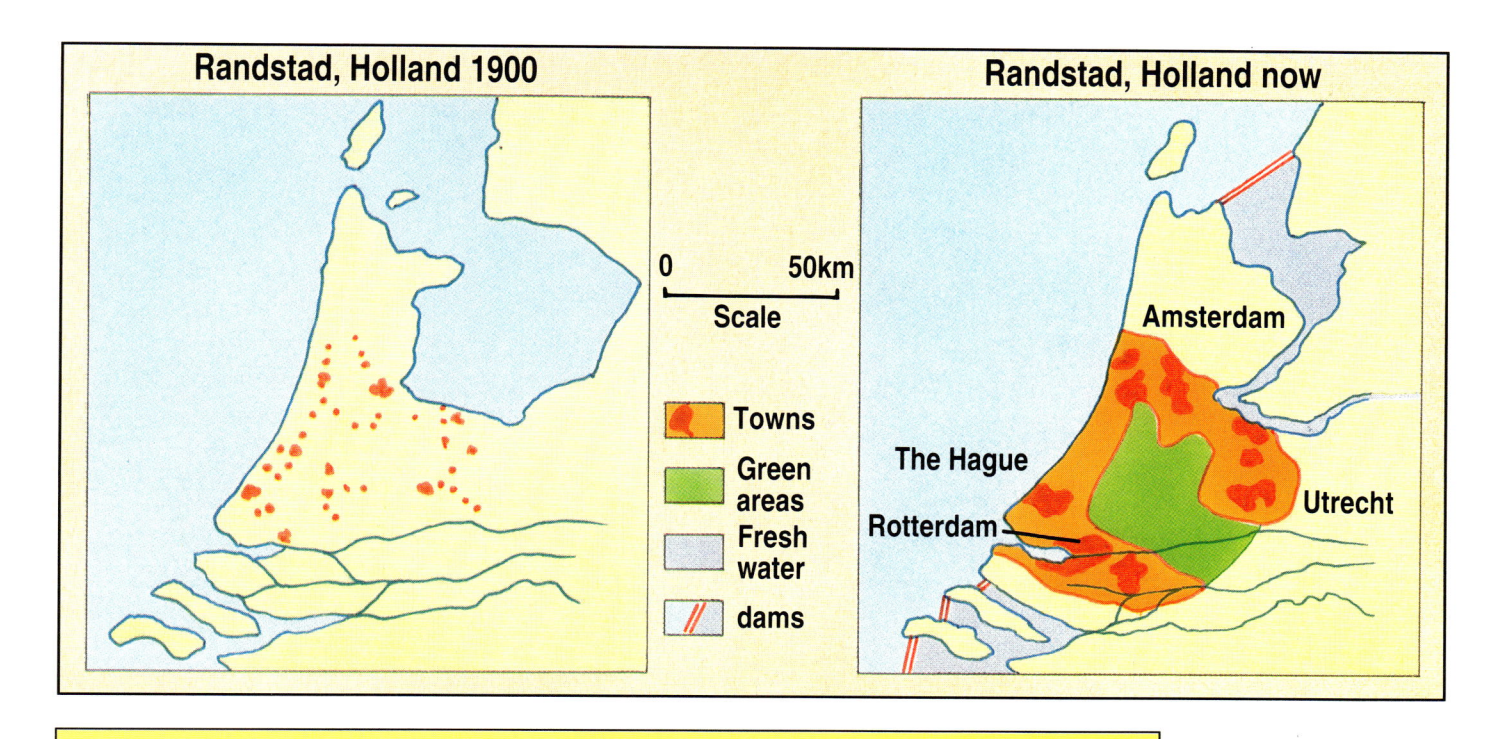

Randstad

Randstad, or 'The Ringed City', is an area in the west of the Netherlands. There are a number of towns and cities within the Randstad.

You can see from the diagram above how much the area has grown since 1900. Randstad covers only 16 per cent of the land in the Netherlands, but 42 per cent of Dutch people live there.

Samarkand

Samarkand is a city in Uzbekistan. The city is home to three groups of people, and is divided into three parts. People who follow the Islamic religion live mainly in the old town. Here, the streets are narrow and the houses have flat roofs. Everywhere you can see the high towers of the mosques, the places of worship of Muslims.

In the Russian new town, the houses are much more modern and the streets are wider.

The third town is the newest and most modern. It was built in 1917.

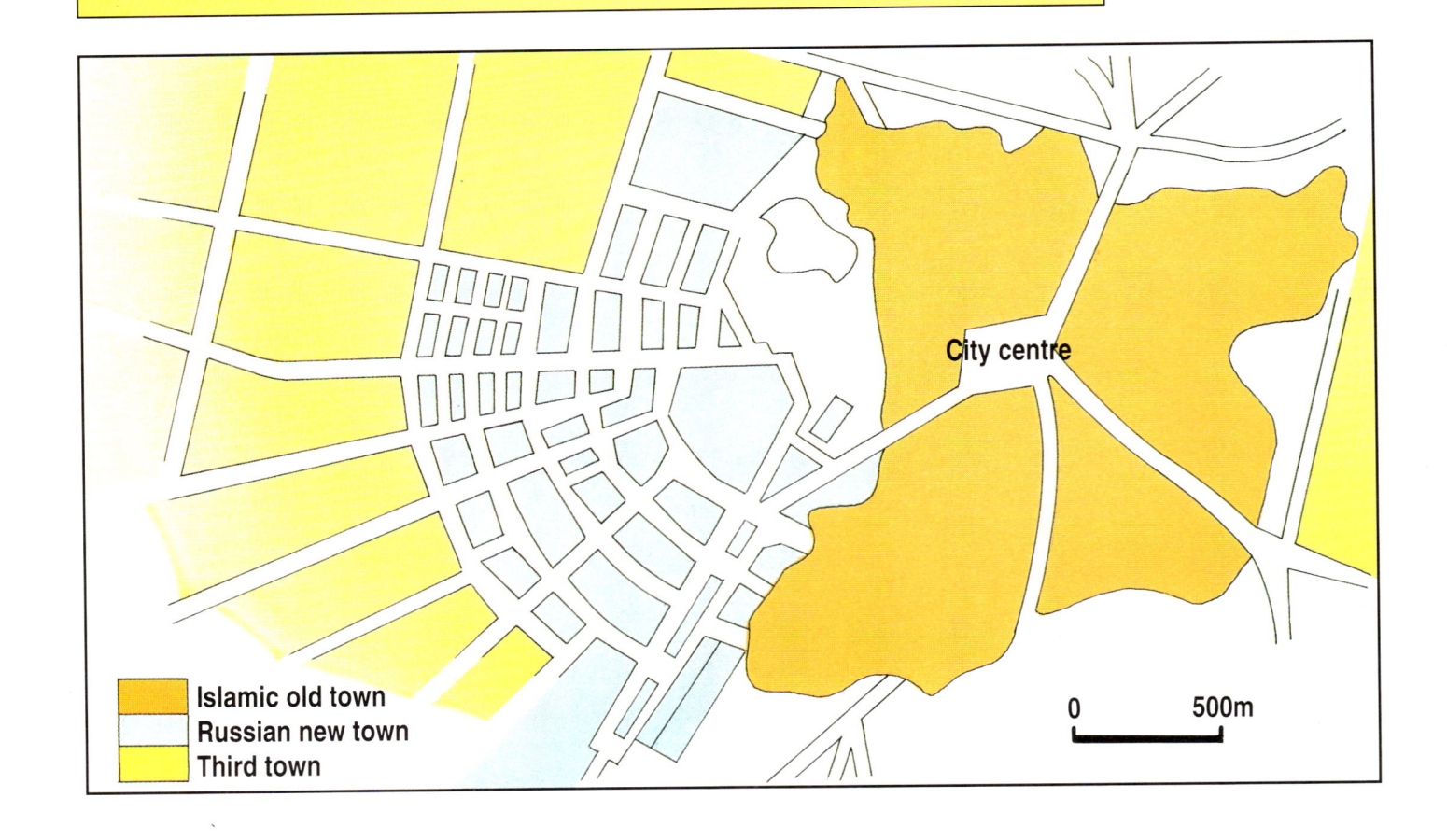

- Islamic old town
- Russian new town
- Third town

City centre

0   500m

Paris is the capital of France. It is a large and beautiful city which is growing all the time. There is a price to pay for this growth, however. The countryside around Paris is suffering the effects of pollution from the city.

The River Seine flows through Paris. Here, we can see the waste and pollution which has been dumped in the river. ▶

◀ This photograph of a housing estate was taken from an aeroplane.

Housing estates have been built on the outskirts of most European cities to solve the problem of overcrowding. However, they are built on land that was once countryside.

How we live

The city of Moscow is growing day by day as more factories and blocks of flats are built. Gradually the city has spread out to take up land from the neighbouring countryside, known as the green belt. ▶

◀ The Sun goes down over a town in Tuscany in Italy. People come from all over the world to visit the beautiful area of Tuscany. However, for the people living in the area, jobs are few and life can be quite hard.

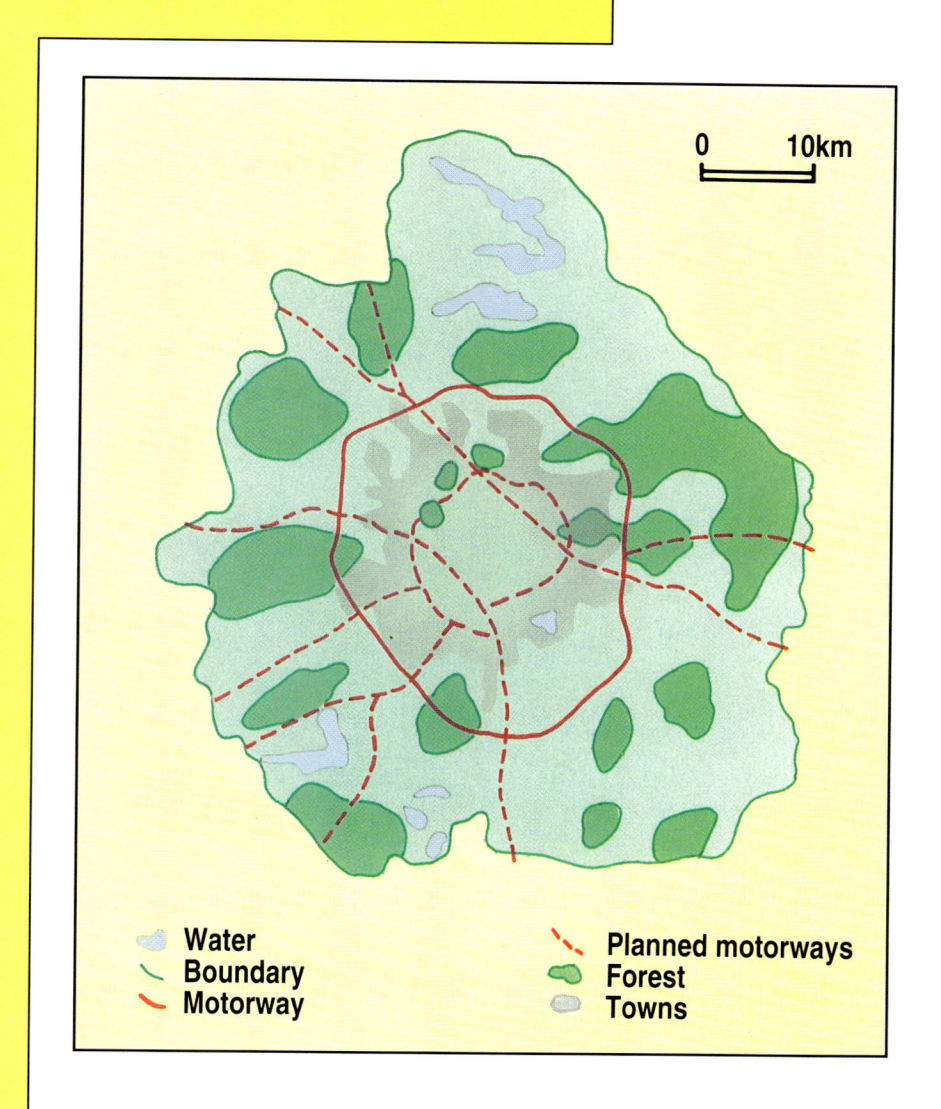

0 10km

Water
Boundary
Motorway
Planned motorways
Forest
Towns

▲ *This famous open-air theatre is in Verona in Italy. Concerts and plays are held here.*

Children recovering at a hospital in Russia. It is important that all people have a good standard of health care. ▶

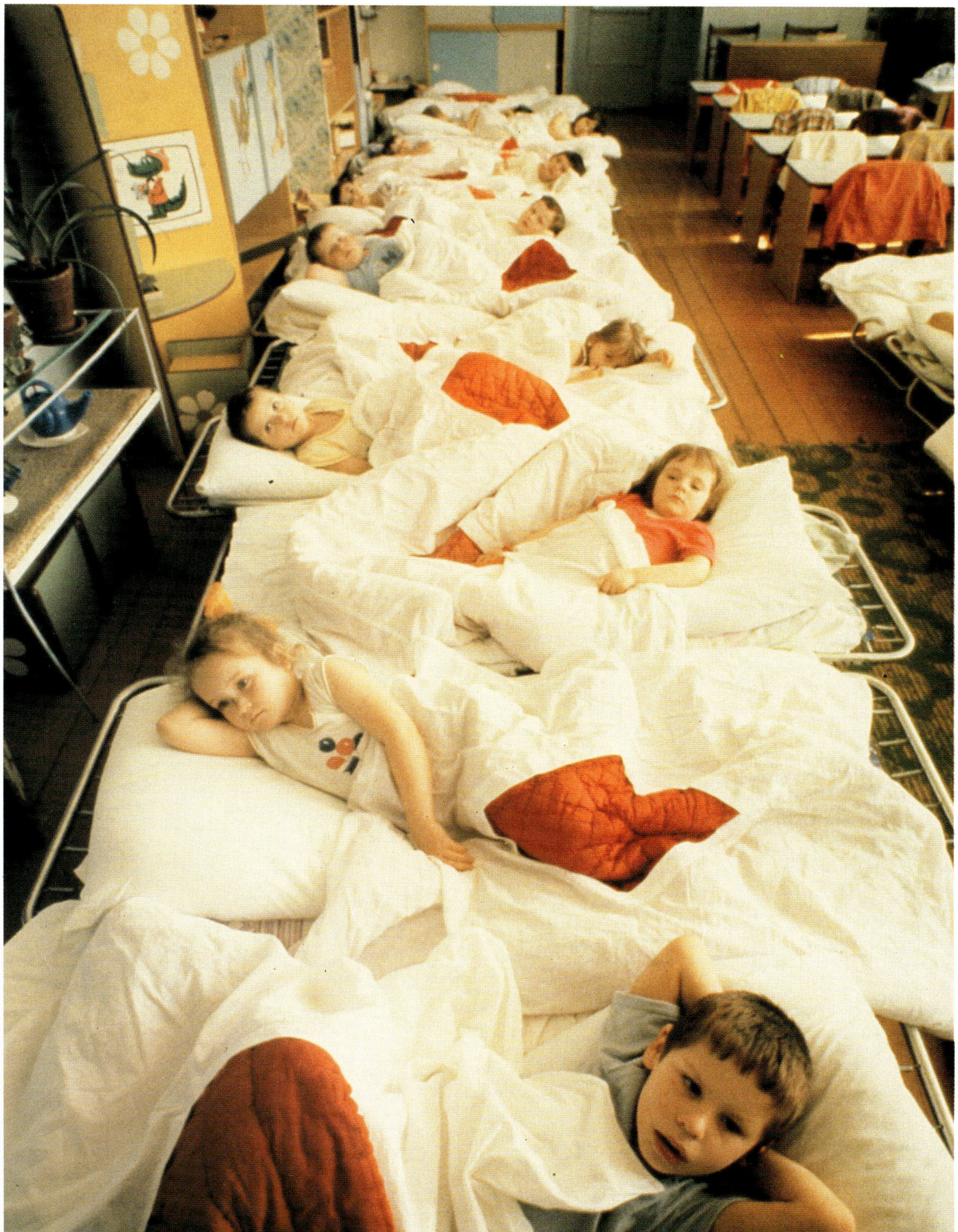

This map shows which countries in Europe have the best quality of life. ▶

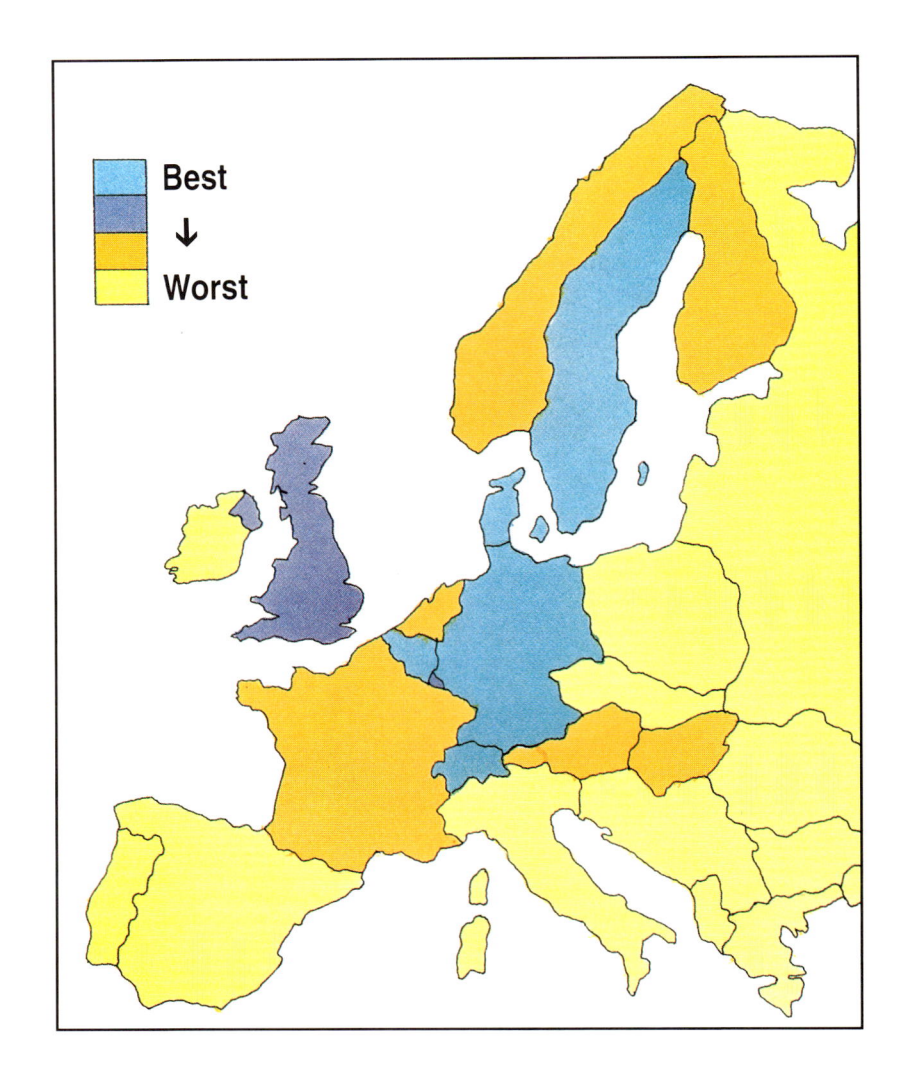

Best
↓
Worst

The photograph at the top of the opposite page shows blocks of flats in Cluj in Romania. Here, people live in cramped, difficult conditions. There are no parks or open spaces nearby where children can play. ▶

Some of the most important things people need to live well are a proper home, education, health care, job opportunities, a clean and safe environment and free time to enjoy sport and hobbies.

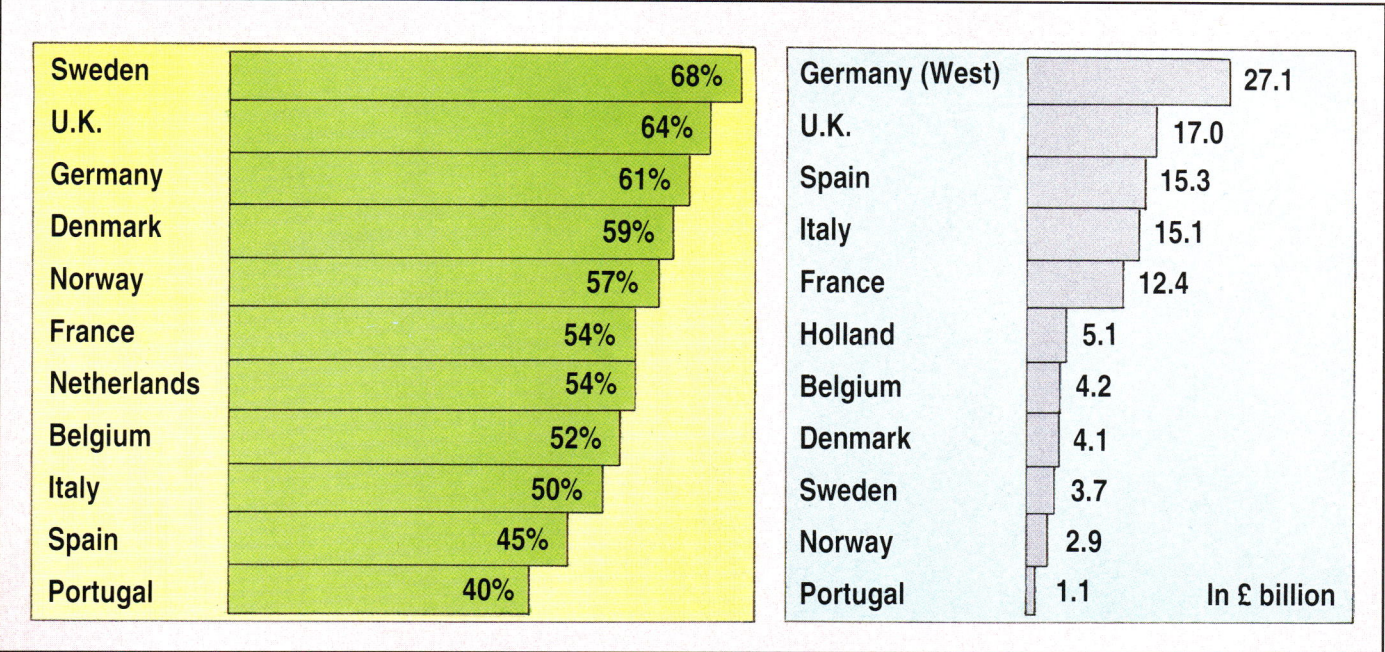

Sweden	68%
U.K.	64%
Germany	61%
Denmark	59%
Norway	57%
France	54%
Netherlands	54%
Belgium	52%
Italy	50%
Spain	45%
Portugal	40%

▲ Families who have a holiday every year.

Germany (West)	27.1
U.K.	17.0
Spain	15.3
Italy	15.1
France	12.4
Holland	5.1
Belgium	4.2
Denmark	4.1
Sweden	3.7
Norway	2.9
Portugal	1.1

In £ billion

▲ People who spend most money on holidays.

43

▲ *It is important that cities have parks and green spaces for us to visit.*

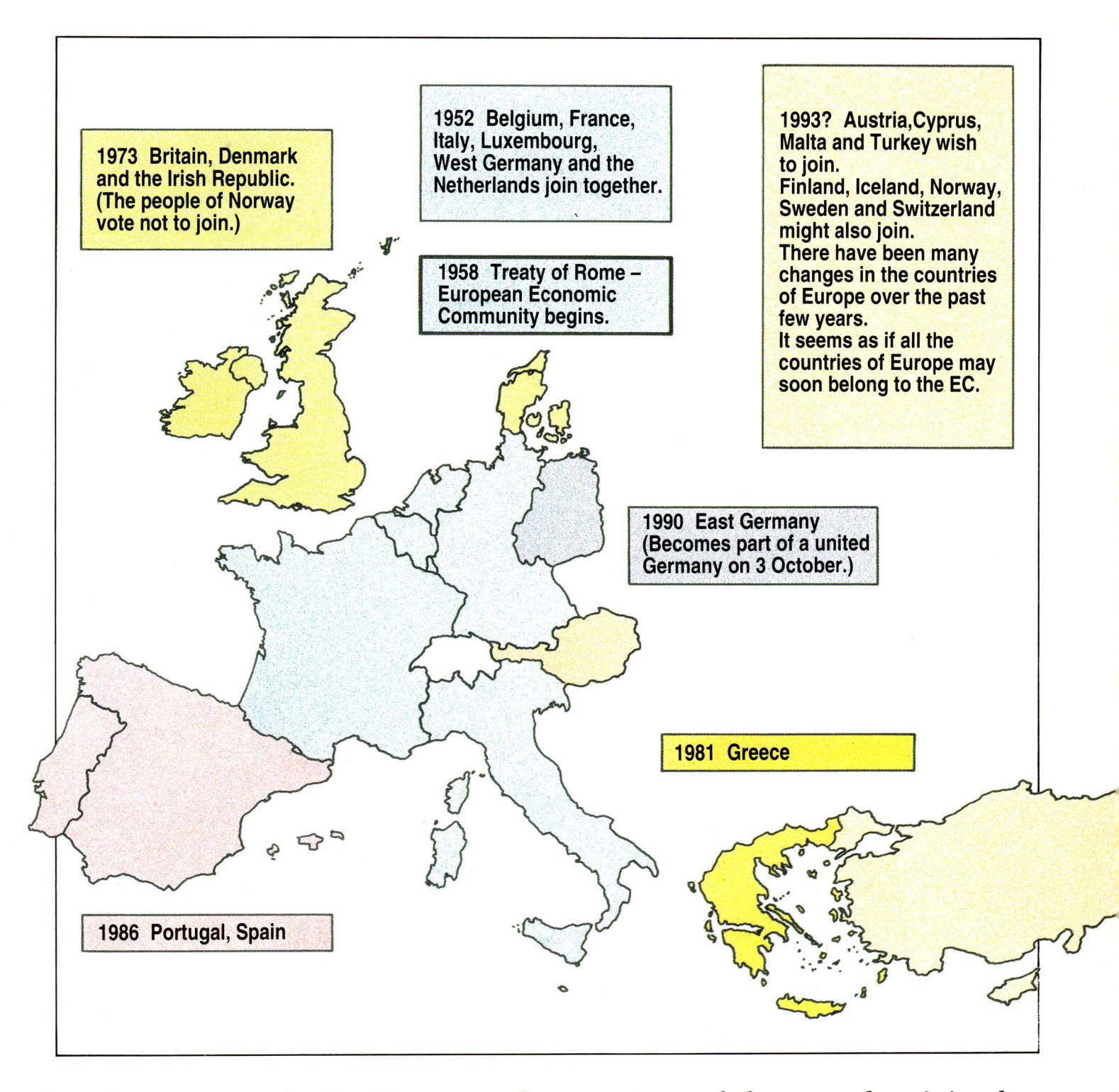

1973 Britain, Denmark and the Irish Republic. (The people of Norway vote not to join.)

1952 Belgium, France, Italy, Luxembourg, West Germany and the Netherlands join together.

1958 Treaty of Rome – European Economic Community begins.

1993? Austria, Cyprus, Malta and Turkey wish to join.
Finland, Iceland, Norway, Sweden and Switzerland might also join.
There have been many changes in the countries of Europe over the past few years.
It seems as if all the countries of Europe may soon belong to the EC.

1990 East Germany (Becomes part of a united Germany on 3 October.)

1981 Greece

1986 Portugal, Spain

▲ *The countries in the European Community and the year they joined.*

45

Glossary

balconies Platforms which jut out from the walls of buildings, where people can sit, hang out washing or plant flowers.

climate The weather in an area or country.

continent One of the five areas into which the world is divided: Africa, Asia, Australia, Europe, North and South America.

environment The world around us. For example, animals, plants, rivers, mountains and the air we breathe.

European Community (EC) A group of countries which have joined together to come up with ideas and plans for energy, farming and industry in Europe.

fertile Able to make things grow.

high-tech (short for high-technology) Very up-to-date machines and methods.

lifestyle How people live their lives: what they eat; where they live; how they spend their free time, for example.

pollution Things that spoil the environment.

population The people, or number of people, who live in a place.

resorts Places where people go on holiday.

turf Short grass and the layer of soil underneath.

More information

Books to read

Food and Drink series (Wayland, 1987)
Greece by Julia Waterlow (Wayland, 1991)
Inside France by Ian James (Franklin Watts, 1988)
Italy by Jillian Powell (Wayland, 1991)
Italy, People and Places by Marylyn Tolhurst (Templar Publishing, 1988)
The United Kingdom by Christa Stadtler (Wayland, 1991)

Further information

If you would like more information on life in Europe, you can write to these organizations.

Commission of the European Communities
8 Storey's Gate
London SW1P 3AT

Council of Europe
Boîte Postale 431 R6
67006 Strasbourg Cedex
France

UNESCO
7 Place de Fontenoy
Paris
France

Index

cities, living in   11, 13, 23, 24, 25, 27, 28-38
   new   33, 36
   the Ruhr   32
climate   6, 7
commuters   24, 27
countryside, living in   11, 13, 22-27, 33
   in Italy   22
   in Russia   25
culture   4, 14, 15

England   27
environment   23, 42

farming   7, 8
France   9, 20, 37

Germany   5, 14, 29, 32
Greece   18, 20
guest workers   14-15

health care and hospitals   4, 5, 11, 13, 23, 40, 42
houses and homes   6, 10, 16-19, 22, 23, 24, 25, 27, 29

Iceland   19
industry   7, 11, 29, 32
Ireland   24
Italy   7-8, 16, 18, 20, 39, 40

landscapes   6, 25
languages   14, 15
lifestyle   38-45

Netherlands, the   17, 20, 33, 35

pollution   10, 13, 32, 37
population   5
Portugal   15, 18, 20

Romania   42
Russia   10, 25, 33-4, 40

schools and education   7, 23, 34, 42
Scotland   23
shops   11, 13, 20-21, 27, 34
Spain   18, 20

tourism   9, 31